KRIS DAVE LAZARTE

The Virtual Assistant Starter Handbook

A Short Guide to Skills, Opportunities, and Making the Decision to Become a VA

Copyright © 2024 by Kris Dave Lazarte

All rights reserved. No part of this publication may be reproduced, stored or transmitted in any form or by any means, electronic, mechanical, photocopying, recording, scanning, or otherwise without written permission from the publisher. It is illegal to copy this book, post it to a website, or distribute it by any other means without permission.

Kris Dave Lazarte asserts the moral right to be identified as the author of this work.

Kris Dave Lazarte has no responsibility for the persistence or accuracy of URLs for external or third-party Internet Websites referred to in this publication and does not guarantee that any content on such Websites is, or will remain, accurate or appropriate.

Designations used by companies to distinguish their products are often claimed as trademarks. All brand names and product names used in this book and on its cover are trade names, service marks, trademarks and registered trademarks of their respective owners. The publishers and the book are not associated with any product or vendor mentioned in this book. None of the companies referenced within the book have endorsed the book.

First edition

*This book was professionally typeset on Reedsy.
Find out more at reedsy.com*

Contents

Introduction	1
My Journey: From Remote Worker to VA	1
Why This Book?	2
Chapter 1: Understanding the Virtual Assistant Role	4
Section 1.1: What is a Virtual Assistant?	4
Definition and Scope of Work	4
Types of Clients You'll Work With	6
Industry Trends and Growth	6
Section 1.2: The Benefits of Becoming a VA	8
Flexibility and Work-Life Balance	8
Diverse Income Opportunities	9
Personal and Professional Growth	10
Section 1.3: Challenges to Expect	11
1. Time Management Issues	11
2. Client Communication Barriers	12
3. Financial and Career Uncertainty	13
Chapter 2: Skills and Tools Every VA Needs	15
Section 2.1: Essential Skills for Success	15
1. Administrative Skills	15
2. Communication Skills	16
3. Technical Skills	16
Bringing It All Together	17
Section 2.2: Must-Have Tools for VAs	18

1. Productivity and Collaboration Tools	18
2. Financial and Invoicing Software	19
3. Marketing and Outreach Platforms	19
Why These Tools Matter	20
Section 2.3: Soft Skills to Develop	20
1. Adaptability	21
2. Problem-Solving	22
3. Self-Motivation	23
Building Your Foundation	23
You're Starting Your Own Business	24
Chapter 3: Exploring Opportunities and Finding Clients	25
Section 3.1: Popular Niches for VAs	25
1. General Administrative VA	25
2. Specialized VA Services	26
3. Industry-Specific VAs	28
Finding Your Perfect Fit	29
Section 3.2: Marketing Yourself as a VA	29
1. Building an Online Presence	29
2. Networking Strategies	30
3. Pitching to Potential Clients	31
Take Action and Market Your VA Business	32
Section 3.3: Platforms to Get Started	32
1. Freelancing Websites	33
2. Job Boards and Remote Work Platforms	33
3. Direct Outreach Methods	34
Take the First Step	35
Chapter 4: Deciding if Becoming a VA is Right for You	36
Section 4.1: Evaluating Your Skills and Goals	36
1. Assessing Your Strengths	36

2. Setting Career Goals	37
3. Understanding Your "Why"	38
Take the Time to Reflect	39
Section 4.2: Planning Your Transition	39
1. Building a Financial Cushion	39
2. Preparing Your Workspace	40
3. Crafting a Clear Roadmap	41
Keep Going—You're Almost There!	42
Section 4.3: Making the Final Decision	42
1. Weighing Pros and Cons	43
2. Conducting a Reality Check	43
3. Taking the Leap	44
You've Done It—Now Decide	45
Conclusion	46

Introduction

Welcome to *The Virtual Assistant Starter Handbook.* Interested in the world of virtual assistants and remote work? This book is for you. Think of it as your guide to understanding the skills, opportunities, and decisions involved in stepping into this exciting profession.

This isn't a long, drawn-out manual. It's a short, focused guide to help you quickly get up to speed. You'll learn what virtual assistants do, what industries they work in, and how they find clients. More importantly, this book is designed to help you answer a crucial question: *Do I have what it takes to become a VA, and do I want to pursue this path?*

By the end of this book, you'll know enough about the world of virtual assistance to make an informed decision. If you decide to move forward, you'll also get practical tips on what to do next—how to build your skills, market yourself, and land your first client.

My Journey: From Remote Worker to VA

I didn't start out as a virtual assistant. My career began in 2011, working remotely for a company in operations. My role wasn't glamorous, but it was rewarding. I managed forums, coordinated with vendors, generated reports, updated user guides, and maintained the company website. In short, I wore many hats, much like a VA does today.

I graduated with a Bachelor of Science in Information and Computer Science, but instead of diving into programming, I found my passion elsewhere—operations and problem-solving. I've always loved working with computers and, even more, helping others understand and use them effectively.

Over time, I realized that the work I enjoyed most involved supporting others, streamlining processes, and solving problems. That's when I saw the potential of virtual assistance—not just as a career but as a way to blend my skills, passions, and the flexibility of remote work.

Why This Book?

Maybe you're curious about what your friend or family member does as a work-from-home VA. Or perhaps you're exploring ways to escape the traditional office grind. Either way, this book will give you a clear understanding of what being a VA is all about.

You'll discover:

- **What a VA does**: From managing emails to coordinating projects, virtual assistants play a crucial role in keeping businesses running smoothly.
- **What industries you can serve**: The opportunities are as diverse as your interests—from real estate to e-commerce, marketing, and beyond.
- **How to get started**: Whether it's building skills, crafting your resume, or connecting with potential clients, this book

will point you in the right direction.

My goal is to help you see the big picture—and the details—so you can decide if this is the right path for you. I'm not here to sell you a dream or sugarcoat the challenges. But if you're ready to explore a flexible, rewarding career that puts you in control of your time and skills, you're in the right place.

So, let's dive in. By the time you finish this book, you'll know exactly what it takes to be a virtual assistant and, more importantly, if it's a career that excites you. Whether you decide to pursue it or not, my hope is that this guide will leave you inspired, informed, and ready to take the next step—whatever that might be for you.

Chapter 1: Understanding the Virtual Assistant Role

Section 1.1: What is a Virtual Assistant?

At its core, a **Virtual Assistant (VA)** is someone who provides professional support services to clients, all from the comfort of their own home—or wherever they choose to work. Virtual assistants handle tasks that are essential to keeping businesses and individuals organized, productive, and on track.

But being a VA isn't just about administrative work. The role is as versatile as the clients you serve. Whether it's managing schedules, creating content, running social media, or organizing data, VAs act as an extra pair of hands, helping their clients focus on what they do best.

Definition and Scope of Work

A VA is a remote worker who provides various services to businesses, entrepreneurs, or busy professionals. The scope of work can vary widely, but some common responsibilities include:

- Booking travel or appointments
- Conducting research
- Creating and managing spreadsheets
- Handling customer support inquiries
- Managing social media accounts (post content with images or carousels, re-post, message, invite connections)
- Assisting with bookkeeping or invoicing
- Create and design Business Proposal PowerPoint and diagrams
- Review and maintain customer agreement templates (version checks, comparisons, updates)
- Create and send holiday greetings email; manage recipient master list
- Write and post blogs or articles online
- Add, create, or edit website pages/posts
- Prepare event materials (presentations, registration forms, attendance reports, communication, and coordination)
- Manage calendar (send invites, create entries)
- Coordinate with agencies, vendors, and departments (Information Security Certification, grants, website cloning, insurance, awards, documentation updates)
- Design physical name cards and vCards with QR codes
- Create and update brochures

Depending on your skills and interests, you can specialize in one area or offer a mix of services. As businesses increasingly rely on digital tools and remote collaboration, the demand for VAs has expanded significantly.

Types of Clients You'll Work With

One of the most exciting aspects of being a VA is the variety of clients you can work with. Each client has unique needs, giving you the chance to explore different industries and build a diverse portfolio. Here are some examples:

- **Entrepreneurs and Small Business Owners:** These clients often need help with managing day-to-day operations, freeing them up to focus on growing their business.
- **Startups:** Fast-paced and innovative, startups frequently rely on VAs to handle tasks like research, scheduling, and team coordination.
- **Corporate Executives:** Busy professionals often hire VAs to organize their personal and professional lives, from managing emails to booking travel.
- **Coaches and Consultants:** These clients may need help with social media management, email marketing, or client onboarding.
- **E-commerce Sellers:** Online store owners often require assistance with inventory management, customer service, and order processing.

Your client base could be as niche or as broad as you want, allowing you to align your work with your interests and expertise.

Industry Trends and Growth

The VA industry is booming, driven by several factors:

1. **Remote Work Revolution:** The shift to remote work has

normalized virtual collaboration, making VAs an integral part of modern business operations.
2. **Growing Need for Flexibility:** Companies are increasingly outsourcing tasks to freelancers and VAs to reduce overhead costs and stay agile.
3. **Technology and Automation:** Digital tools have made it easier for VAs to manage tasks, communicate with clients, and deliver results efficiently.
4. **Global Accessibility:** With the internet bridging geographical gaps, clients can now hire skilled VAs from anywhere in the world, creating opportunities for professionals in every corner of the globe.

According to industry reports, the demand for virtual assistants is expected to grow steadily in the coming years. This trend isn't just about cost-saving—it's about finding talented, adaptable professionals who can seamlessly integrate into a team, no matter where they're located.

As you can see, being a VA is about more than just working from home. It's about embracing a dynamic and evolving profession that offers flexibility, variety, and the chance to work with incredible people and businesses. Whether you're drawn to the freedom, the opportunities, or simply the chance to do meaningful work, the VA world is ready for you to explore.

Section 1.2: The Benefits of Becoming a VA

Choosing to become a Virtual Assistant (VA) offers more than just a way to work remotely. It's a chance to build a career that aligns with your personal values, goals, and lifestyle. Whether you're looking for flexibility, a diverse income stream, or an opportunity for growth, being a VA can provide all of this and more. Let's dive into the top benefits of becoming a VA.

Flexibility and Work-Life Balance

One of the most appealing benefits of being a VA is the **flexibility** it offers. As a VA, you're in control of your schedule. No more 9-to-5 office grind. You can set your own working hours based on when you feel most productive and when your clients need you.

This flexibility allows you to better balance your personal and professional life. Need to run errands during the day? Want to take a long weekend trip? As long as you manage your time effectively and communicate with your clients, you have the freedom to make your work fit into your life.

For many VAs, this flexibility means:

- **More family time:** You can schedule your work around family commitments.
- **Work from anywhere:** As long as you have an internet connection, you can work from virtually anywhere in the world.
- **Better health and well-being:** The ability to take breaks when needed or create a comfortable work environment can lead to reduced stress and improved mental health.

Diverse Income Opportunities

The beauty of being a VA is the **diverse income opportunities** available to you. You're not tied to one job or one source of income. As a VA, you can choose to work with multiple clients or specialize in a niche area that allows you to charge higher rates. Here's how this diversity can work in your favor:

- **Hourly vs. Retainer Rates**: Some clients may prefer to pay on an hourly basis, while others may choose a monthly retainer. Retainers provide steady income, while hourly work can allow you to scale your income based on how much you want to work.
- **Specializing in a Niche**: Specializing in areas like social media management, content creation, or technical support can allow you to charge premium rates.
- **Upselling Services**: As you gain experience, you may find that clients want additional services that you can offer, such as creating a website, managing online marketing campaigns, or even providing training.
- **Global Reach**: Being a remote worker means your clients aren't limited by geography. You can work with anyone, anywhere, which opens up a world of opportunities.

With the right skills, your income as a VA can grow exponentially. Plus, you have the freedom to decide how much or how little you want to work.

Personal and Professional Growth

Working as a VA isn't just a job—it's a **path to personal and professional growth**. Here are just a few ways this career can help you grow:

- **Skill Development**: As a VA, you'll continually develop new skills, whether it's mastering a new software tool, improving your communication, or learning to manage multiple projects. These skills not only make you more valuable to clients, but they also increase your marketability in the long run.
- **Independence and Confidence**: Being a successful VA means managing your own business, setting your rates, and finding clients. This fosters a sense of independence and boosts your confidence as you navigate new challenges and opportunities.
- **Work Variety**: Every client and every task is different. As a VA, you'll rarely be bored. You'll learn about different industries, tackle new challenges, and develop a wide-ranging skill set.
- **Networking Opportunities**: As you work with different clients, you'll expand your professional network, which can lead to new job opportunities, collaborations, and even potential mentorships.
- **Job Satisfaction**: Many VAs find that the satisfaction of helping others manage their workload and achieve their goals gives them a deep sense of fulfillment. The work you do truly matters, and you can see the positive impact you have on your clients' success.

Section 1.3: Challenges to Expect

Like any career, becoming a Virtual Assistant (VA) comes with its challenges. While the benefits are numerous, it's important to prepare for potential obstacles so you can navigate them with confidence. Here are three common challenges you may face as a VA—and strategies to overcome them.

1. Time Management Issues

When you're in charge of your schedule, managing your time effectively can be a double-edged sword. Without a structured office environment or fixed hours, it's easy to underestimate how long tasks will take or to overcommit yourself.

Common struggles include:

- Balancing multiple clients with competing deadlines.
- Allowing work to bleed into personal time.
- Staying focused when distractions arise at home.

How to overcome it:

- **Set Clear Boundaries**: Establish specific working hours and communicate them to your clients. Use tools like time-tracking apps to keep yourself accountable.
- **Prioritize Tasks**: Start each day by identifying your top priorities and tackling them first. The Eisenhower Matrix (urgent vs. important tasks) can be a helpful framework.
- **Use a Scheduling System**: Tools like Google Calendar,

Trello, or Asana can help you organize tasks and deadlines across different clients.

Remember, good time management isn't about being perfect—it's about finding systems that work for you and adjusting as needed.

2. Client Communication Barriers

Working remotely means that almost all communication happens through email, chat, or video calls. Miscommunication can happen when messages are unclear, cultural differences arise, or expectations aren't aligned.

Common struggles include:

- Misunderstanding client instructions.
- Delayed responses that slow down progress.
- Navigating language or cultural differences with international clients.

How to overcome it:

- **Clarify Expectations Early**: At the start of each project, discuss timelines, deliverables, and preferred communication methods. Summarize key points in writing to avoid misunderstandings.
- **Be Proactive**: If you're unsure about something, ask questions right away. Regularly update clients on your progress to show accountability.

- **Invest in Communication Tools**: Platforms like Slack, Zoom, or Microsoft Teams can facilitate smoother, real-time collaboration.
- **Improve Your Skills**: Take courses or read guides on effective written and verbal communication to enhance your ability to express ideas clearly.

Great communication builds trust, which is essential for maintaining long-term client relationships.

3. Financial and Career Uncertainty

As a VA, you're essentially running your own business, which means income can fluctuate. There may be months when clients cut back on hours or when you need to hustle harder to find new work. This uncertainty can feel daunting, especially when you're just starting out.

Common struggles include:

- Inconsistent income streams.
- Difficulty securing long-term clients.
- Lack of clear career progression compared to traditional jobs.

How to overcome it:

- **Diversify Your Client Base**: Relying on a single client for your income can be risky. Aim to have a mix of short-term and long-term clients to balance your workload.

- **Save for Lean Times**: Build an emergency fund to cover expenses during slow months. Many VAs aim to save three to six months of living expenses.
- **Set Realistic Rates**: Research industry standards and price your services accordingly. Don't undervalue your work—charging fair rates ensures your business remains sustainable.
- **Invest in Your Future**: As you grow, consider adding new skills or certifications that allow you to charge higher rates or specialize in high-demand niches.

Uncertainty is part of the journey, but with careful planning and adaptability, you can create a stable and rewarding VA career.

While these challenges may seem intimidating, they're also opportunities to grow. Every successful VA faces obstacles along the way—it's how you handle them that defines your journey. With preparation, the right mindset, and a willingness to learn, you'll be well-equipped to overcome these hurdles and thrive in your role as a virtual assistant.

Chapter 2: Skills and Tools Every VA Needs

Section 2.1: Essential Skills for Success

As a Virtual Assistant, your skillset is your superpower. Clients depend on you to make their lives easier, so mastering certain key abilities will set you apart from the competition. Here's a breakdown of the essential skills you'll need to succeed in this dynamic role.

1. Administrative Skills

Administrative tasks are the backbone of a Virtual Assistant's work. These skills ensure smooth operations for your clients:

- **Time Management**: Effectively prioritize and juggle multiple tasks to meet deadlines.
- **Organization**: Maintain order in your client's calendar, emails, and projects. A well-organized VA is invaluable.
- **Attention to Detail**: Spotting errors, managing documents, and keeping track of specifics show your professionalism.

- **Problem-Solving**: Quickly address issues and find solutions without needing constant oversight.

Strong administrative skills are often the first thing clients look for, so honing these abilities is crucial.

2. Communication Skills

Clear and effective communication builds trust with your clients and ensures tasks are completed to their expectations. Here's what to focus on:

- **Professional Writing**: Craft emails, reports, or updates that are concise and polished.
- **Active Listening**: Understand your client's needs by listening carefully and asking thoughtful questions.
- **Virtual Collaboration**: Use tools like Slack, Zoom, or Microsoft Teams to communicate effectively in a remote environment.
- **Empathy and Patience**: Maintaining a positive and understanding tone goes a long way when dealing with clients and their customers.

Great communication can make or break a client relationship, so it's worth mastering this skill early on.

3. Technical Skills

As a VA, you'll often work with digital tools and platforms. Being tech-savvy helps you stand out and take on more advanced tasks. Key technical skills include:

- **Familiarity with Office Software**: Proficiency in tools like Microsoft Office, Google Workspace, or similar platforms is essential.
- **Project Management Tools**: Learn software like Trello, Asana, or ClickUp to manage tasks and collaborate effectively.
- **Basic Website Management**: Understanding platforms like WordPress or Shopify can make you a go-to resource for website updates.
- **Social Media Tools**: Knowing how to schedule posts or analyze engagement using tools like Buffer or Hootsuite is highly valuable.
- **Adaptability to New Tech**: The ability to quickly learn new software or systems is one of the most prized skills in a VA.

Bringing It All Together

Success as a Virtual Assistant comes down to mastering a mix of administrative, communication, and technical skills. But don't worry—no one starts out perfect. The key is to build your abilities step by step, focusing on the areas where you excel while learning new skills as needed.

By investing in these essential skills, you'll not only meet client expectations—you'll exceed them. And that's how you build a successful and sustainable career as a Virtual Assistant.

- Using productivity software (e.g., Google Workspace, Microsoft Office)
- Basic graphic design (e.g., Canva, Photoshop)

- Knowledge of CMS platforms (e.g., WordPress)

Section 2.2: Must-Have Tools for VAs

Equipping yourself with the right tools is essential to thrive as a Virtual Assistant. These tools streamline your workflow, help you stay organized, and make your services more efficient and professional. Here's a breakdown of the must-have tools every VA should know about.

1. Productivity and Collaboration Tools

As a VA, you'll juggle multiple tasks and collaborate remotely with clients. These tools are vital for staying organized and maintaining clear communication:

- **Task Management**: Use tools like Trello, Asana, or ClickUp to organize projects, set deadlines, and track progress.
- **Scheduling**: Simplify calendar management with apps like Google Calendar or Calendly to coordinate meetings effortlessly.
- **File Sharing**: Tools like Google Drive and Dropbox ensure seamless sharing and storage of documents.
- **Communication Platforms**: Stay connected with clients using Zoom, Slack, or Microsoft Teams for video calls and messaging.

These tools not only make your work easier but also demonstrate your professionalism and tech-savviness to clients.

2. Financial and Invoicing Software

Managing your finances is a critical part of running your VA business. The right tools can help you track income, send invoices, and stay on top of taxes:

- **Invoicing Tools**: Platforms like FreshBooks, QuickBooks, or Wave make it easy to create and send professional invoices.
- **Payment Processors**: Use PayPal, Stripe, or Wise to receive payments securely from clients worldwide.
- **Expense Tracking**: Keep tabs on your expenses with tools like Mint or Expensify for accurate budgeting and tax preparation.
- **Time Tracking**: Tools like Toggl or Harvest help you log hours for projects and ensure accurate billing.

By managing your finances effectively, you'll maintain a stable and professional operation that builds client trust.

3. Marketing and Outreach Platforms

Finding and securing clients is a vital part of growing your VA career. These tools can help you market your services and connect with potential clients:

- **Social Media Management**: Use platforms like Buffer or Hootsuite to schedule and analyze posts across social media

accounts.
- **Portfolio Websites**: Create an online portfolio with tools like Wix, Squarespace, or Canva to showcase your skills and services.
- **Freelance Platforms**: Explore sites like Upwork, Fiverr, or LinkedIn to find job opportunities and connect with clients.
- **Email Marketing**: Tools like Mailchimp or ConvertKit help you maintain communication with prospects and past clients.

Building your online presence and reaching out to potential clients becomes much easier with these platforms in your toolkit.

Why These Tools Matter

Having the right tools is more than just a convenience—it's a way to demonstrate your efficiency, stay organized, and deliver outstanding results for your clients. Don't worry if you're unfamiliar with some of these platforms; most are user-friendly, and with a bit of practice, you'll become proficient in no time.

Remember, being a VA is about working smarter, not harder. The right tools will help you do just that.

Section 2.3: Soft Skills to Develop

Success as a Virtual Assistant goes beyond just the technical or administrative skills you bring to the table—although those are important too. It's also about mastering the soft skills that really make a difference. Think about your ability to adapt to new situations, solve problems creatively, and keep yourself motivated even when things get tough. These soft skills are what set you apart and help you truly thrive in this dynamic role. They're the foundation that supports everything you do, helping you build strong relationships with clients and stay on top of your game. Remember, it's your resilience, adaptability, and passion that will carry you forward. You've got what it takes, and I'm excited to see you succeed!

1. Adaptability

In the world of virtual assistance, change is the only constant. New tools, shifting client needs, and evolving industries mean you need to be flexible and open to change.

Why It Matters:

- Clients value a VA who can quickly adjust to new processes or unexpected challenges without missing a beat.

How to Develop It:

- Embrace learning by staying updated on trends and tools in your industry.
- Practice staying calm under pressure when priorities shift unexpectedly.
- Approach challenges as opportunities to grow and expand your expertise.

By staying adaptable, you'll position yourself as a reliable partner who can handle anything your clients throw at you.

2. Problem-Solving

As a VA, you'll often be the go-to person for fixing issues or finding solutions. Problem-solving skills are crucial for tackling tasks efficiently and earning your client's trust.

Why It Matters:

- Clients need someone who doesn't just identify problems but takes initiative to solve them.

How to Develop It:

- Break problems into smaller, manageable steps to avoid feeling overwhelmed.
- Research solutions independently before seeking help, showing resourcefulness.
- Learn from past challenges and apply those lessons to future situations.

Problem-solving not only makes you invaluable to your clients but also builds your confidence in handling complex tasks.

3. Self-Motivation

Working remotely requires discipline and a strong sense of motivation. Without a boss looking over your shoulder, staying on track is entirely up to you.

Why It Matters:

- Your ability to manage your time and meet deadlines independently will directly impact your reputation and success.

How to Develop It:

- Set clear daily and weekly goals to give yourself direction and purpose.
- Celebrate small wins to stay energized and maintain momentum.
- Create a dedicated workspace free from distractions to maintain focus.

Self-motivation allows you to take charge of your career and build the kind of work-life balance you've always wanted.

Building Your Foundation

Soft skills are often overlooked, but they are just as important—if not more so—than the technical skills you bring to the table. The good news is that these abilities aren't fixed traits. With practice, you can strengthen your adaptability, problem-solving, and self-motivation, paving the way for a fulfilling and successful career as a Virtual Assistant.

Developing these soft skills will set you apart and give you the confidence to tackle any challenge that comes your way.

You're Starting Your Own Business

Becoming a Virtual Assistant isn't just about working for someone else—it's like starting your own business. You're in charge of managing your time, your services, and your clients. The path to success won't always be easy, but with hard work, dedication, and the development of these soft skills, you can build a rewarding and flexible career.

Success in business doesn't come overnight. It takes effort, persistence, and a willingness to grow. Embrace the challenges that come with this journey, and know that with every step, you're building a foundation for a thriving business and a fulfilling career.

You've got this!

Chapter 3: Exploring Opportunities and Finding Clients

Section 3.1: Popular Niches for VAs

One of the greatest advantages of being a Virtual Assistant is the flexibility to specialize in areas that align with your skills, interests, and passions. Whether you prefer variety or want to focus on a specific expertise, there's a niche for everyone. Here's an overview of the most popular niches for VAs.

1. General Administrative VA

If you're a multitasker who loves staying organized and helping others stay on track, this is a great starting point. General Administrative VAs handle a wide range of tasks to support clients' day-to-day operations.

Typical Tasks:

- Managing emails and calendars
- Scheduling appointments
- Organizing files and documents
- Data entry and reporting

Who Hires General Admin VAs?

- Entrepreneurs and small business owners
- Busy professionals needing help with time management

This is an excellent niche for those starting out, as the skills required are universal and easy to build upon.

2. Specialized VA Services

If you have expertise in a particular area, offering specialized services allows you to stand out and command higher rates.

Examples of Specialized Niches:

- **Social Media Management**: Creating, scheduling, managing LinkedIn content strategy, engagement, connection outreach and analyzing social media content.
- **Graphic Design**: Designing marketing materials, logos, or social media graphics.
- **Bookkeeping**: Handling financial records and managing budgets.
- **Email Marketing**: Setting up campaigns, managing newsletters, crafting personalized holiday greetings, managing recipient master lists and tracking analytics.

- **E-commerce Support**: Managing online stores, inventory, and customer inquiries.
- **Presentation and Proposal Design:** Creating impactful PowerPoint presentations, business proposals, and visual diagrams.
- **Contract and Agreement Management:** Reviewing, maintaining, and updating agreements and customer templates.
- **Content Creation and Publishing:** Writing and publishing blogs, articles, and website content.
- **Event Coordination and Logistics:** Organizing event materials, communication, and attendance tracking.
- **Calendar and Scheduling:** Managing calendar invites, scheduling, and coordination.
- **Interagency and Vendor Coordination:** Facilitating collaboration for certifications, grants, websites, insurance, and awards.
- **Document and User Guide:** Updating and managing documentation for security, release notes, and guides.
- **Branding and Collateral Design:** Designing brochures, name cards, and digital vCards with QR codes.

Why Specialize?

- Specialization allows you to target clients in need of specific expertise.
- You can charge premium rates for your services.

Specialized niches are perfect if you enjoy diving deep into a particular skill or industry.

3. Industry-Specific VAs

Tailoring your services to a specific industry can set you apart from generalists and build your reputation within a focused market.

Examples of Industry Niches:

- **Real Estate VAs**: Managing listings, scheduling showings, and handling client communication for real estate agents.
- **Legal VAs**: Assisting lawyers with case research, document preparation, and scheduling.
- **Medical VAs**: Supporting medical practices with appointment scheduling, billing, and patient records.
- **Coaching and Consulting VAs**: Helping coaches and consultants manage client onboarding, scheduling, and materials.

Advantages of Industry-Specific Niches:

- Clients value your familiarity with their industry's unique needs.
- You can build expertise and referrals within a specific market.

Choosing an industry-specific niche allows you to become the go-to expert for clients in that field.

Finding Your Perfect Fit

The key to selecting the right niche is identifying where your skills, interests, and market demand overlap. Whether you thrive on variety as a General Administrative VA, enjoy focusing on a specialty, or want to become a sought-after expert in an industry, there's a niche waiting for you.

Remember: your niche isn't set in stone. Many VAs start broad and refine their focus as they gain experience and discover what they love most. The possibilities are endless—start exploring and carve out your unique path!

Section 3.2: Marketing Yourself as a VA

As a Virtual Assistant, marketing yourself effectively is key to building a successful and sustainable career. Whether you're just starting out or looking to grow your business, promoting your skills and services is essential. Here's how to get noticed and attract clients.

1. Building an Online Presence

In today's digital world, your online presence is often the first impression potential clients will have of you. It's your digital handshake—your chance to say, "Hello, I'm here, and I'm ready to help." Establishing a professional and visible online persona isn't just about looking good; it's about standing out from the crowd and building trust with those who need your services.

- **Create a Portfolio Website**: A well-designed website showcases your services, experience, and past work. It's a great way to make a professional impression.
- **Leverage Social Media**: Use platforms like LinkedIn, Instagram, or Facebook to share your expertise, connect with potential clients, and stay top of mind.
- **Start a Blog or Vlog**: Sharing valuable insights related to virtual assistance (or your niche) will demonstrate your expertise and help you attract organic traffic.
- **Claim Your Profiles on Freelance Platforms**: Platforms like Upwork, Fiverr, and Freelancer can help you reach clients searching for specific VA services.

Your online presence is your digital business card. Make sure it reflects the skills and value you offer.

2. Networking Strategies

Networking is about building relationships, not just collecting contacts. Strong, genuine connections can lead to referrals, collaborations, and new opportunities.

- **Join Online Communities**: Participate in groups on LinkedIn, Facebook, or specialized forums related to your niche or virtual assistance in general.
- **Attend Virtual Events and Webinars**: Many industries host virtual meetups, webinars, and conferences where you can connect with potential clients and other VAs.
- **Collaborate with Other Freelancers**: Partner with freelancers in complementary fields (like web designers or

marketers) to expand your reach and gain mutual referrals.
- **Use Client Testimonials**: Word-of-mouth marketing is powerful. Request testimonials from satisfied clients and share them on your website and social media.

Networking helps build a reputation and trust within your industry, which is essential for gaining clients.

3. Pitching to Potential Clients

Once you've built a solid online presence and networked with potential leads, it's time to pitch your services. Crafting a strong pitch can make the difference between a missed opportunity and a new client.

- **Tailor Your Pitch**: Customize each pitch to address the client's specific needs and how you can help solve their problems.
- **Focus on Value, Not Just Skills**: Explain how your services will save them time, increase efficiency, or help them grow. Show them the value you bring.
- **Keep It Concise and Clear**: Busy clients appreciate a brief, to-the-point pitch that highlights your skills and how you can help.
- **Follow Up**: If you don't hear back, send a polite follow-up email to keep the conversation going and show your enthusiasm.

Effective pitching is about demonstrating that you understand the client's needs and showing how your services will help them achieve their goals.

Take Action and Market Your VA Business

Marketing yourself as a VA doesn't have to be intimidating. By building a strong online presence, networking with the right people, and crafting pitches that showcase your value, you'll be on the path to attracting the right clients.

Remember, the key is consistency. Keep putting yourself out there, stay active, and continue to refine your approach. As you build your reputation and network, the clients will follow.

I know this might seem daunting at first, especially if you're not used to putting yourself out there. But trust me, there is no better product to sell than yourself. You've got unique skills, experiences, and personality that no one else can replicate. By taking the time to polish your online profiles, share your expertise, and showcase who you are, you're making that all-important first impression count.

Section 3.3: Platforms to Get Started

When you're ready to start your career as a Virtual Assistant, having the right platforms at your disposal is crucial. Whether you prefer working with established freelance marketplaces, browsing job boards, or reaching out directly to potential clients, there are plenty of avenues to explore. Here's a breakdown of some of the best platforms to help you get started.

CHAPTER 3: EXPLORING OPPORTUNITIES AND FINDING CLIENTS

1. Freelancing Websites

Freelance marketplaces are a great place to begin your VA career. They connect you with clients actively seeking virtual assistants, making it easier to get started, especially if you're new to the industry.

- **Upwork**: A leading platform with a wide variety of jobs, from general administrative tasks to more specialized roles. It's a great place to start building your portfolio.
- **Fiverr**: Perfect for offering specific services, such as social media management, data entry, or scheduling. This platform allows you to set up "gigs" and attract clients looking for targeted services.
- **Freelancer**: Similar to Upwork, with a broad range of job opportunities. You can bid on projects and showcase your experience to stand out.
- **PeoplePerHour**: A platform that allows you to connect with clients seeking hourly services, ideal for VAs looking for flexible, short-term contracts.

Freelancing websites help you tap into an established market of clients actively looking for VA support, giving you an immediate opportunity to start gaining experience.

2. Job Boards and Remote Work Platforms

In addition to freelancing platforms, there are many job boards and remote work platforms where clients post open virtual assistant positions. These platforms often have long-term, stable opportunities.

- **We Work Remotely**: A popular site for finding remote positions across a wide range of industries. Many companies look for VAs to support their teams on an ongoing basis.
- **FlexJobs**: This platform offers a curated list of remote and flexible jobs, ensuring the opportunities are legitimate and high-quality.
- **Remote.co**: A great place to find remote job listings, with a specific focus on roles that can be done from anywhere in the world.
- **Virtual Assistant Jobs**: A niche job board specifically designed for virtual assistants. It lists a variety of positions, from short-term projects to full-time VA roles.

These platforms can help you find both full-time and part-time VA positions, giving you access to employers who are ready to hire.

3. Direct Outreach Methods

While platforms are a great starting point, direct outreach can often lead to more personalized, high-quality opportunities. Building relationships with potential clients is a proactive way to get started.

- **Research Potential Clients**: Look for small business owners, startups, or entrepreneurs who could benefit from your services. Check their websites and social media profiles to identify gaps in their operations that you can help fill.

- **Email Outreach**: Send personalized emails introducing yourself and your services. Tailor your message to highlight how you can solve specific problems they might be facing.
- **Social Media Networking**: Use LinkedIn or Instagram to engage with businesses or individuals who could use a VA. Join groups, participate in discussions, and share valuable content to get noticed.
- **Word of Mouth**: Don't underestimate the power of referrals. Let your friends, family, and acquaintances know you're offering VA services—many of your first clients may come from personal connections.

Direct outreach allows you to build stronger relationships with potential clients and gives you more control over the type of work you take on.

Take the First Step

The key to starting your VA career is taking action. Whether you choose to join a freelancing platform, explore job boards, or reach out directly to businesses, the opportunities are out there.

Get started today by creating profiles on the platforms that resonate with you, reaching out to potential clients, and taking the first steps toward building your client base. Every opportunity you explore brings you closer to building a successful virtual assistant business.

Chapter 4: Deciding if Becoming a VA is Right for You

Section 4.1: Evaluating Your Skills and Goals

Deciding whether becoming a Virtual Assistant is the right path for you requires some introspection. It's not just about having the technical skills; it's about aligning your strengths, personal goals, and motivations with the demands of the role. This section will help you assess whether a VA career is a good fit and how to move forward with clarity and confidence.

1. Assessing Your Strengths

Take time to reflect on your existing skills and personal qualities. The work of a VA spans many areas, from administrative tasks to specialized services, so it's important to recognize where you excel.

- **What tasks do you enjoy?**: Consider past work or personal projects that made you feel accomplished. Do you enjoy

organizing, writing, managing schedules, or solving problems?
- **What are your strengths?**: Are you detail-oriented, efficient, or tech-savvy? Strong organizational skills, communication abilities, and tech fluency are key for a successful VA.
- **What areas need improvement?**: Be honest with yourself. Identifying gaps in your skills (like advanced software knowledge or time management) will help you focus on what to learn next.

Recognizing your strengths—and acknowledging areas for growth—helps you determine if the role of a VA plays to your natural abilities.

2. Setting Career Goals

Your career goals will guide your decision-making and the path you take as a VA. Understanding what you want to achieve is crucial to ensuring you're making the right choice.

- **What do you want to achieve as a VA?**: Do you want a flexible side hustle, a full-time business, or an opportunity to specialize in a certain niche? Setting clear, specific goals will keep you focused and motivated.
- **Short-term goals**: Start by identifying smaller, achievable milestones, like building your online presence, landing your first client, or mastering a new tool or skill.
- **Long-term goals**: Think about where you want to be in one year, five years, or ten years. Do you want to scale your VA

business, hire a team, or become an expert in a particular niche?

By setting clear goals, you'll have a roadmap to follow and a sense of purpose as you build your VA career.

3. Understanding Your "Why"

Knowing *why* you want to become a VA is key to staying motivated, especially during challenging moments. Your personal "why" will drive you through the highs and lows of entrepreneurship.

- **Why do you want to be a VA?**: Do you crave the flexibility of remote work? Are you looking for a way to help others while using your skills? Maybe you want to create a career that gives you more freedom and control over your time.
- **What motivates you?**: Understanding the deeper reasons behind your decision will help you stay committed to your goals.
- **How will this align with your life?**: Will becoming a VA allow you to balance work and personal life more effectively? Will it help you achieve financial independence, creative freedom, or something else entirely?

Your "why" will keep you grounded and focused as you embark on this journey, making it easier to push through obstacles.

Take the Time to Reflect

Becoming a Virtual Assistant is an exciting opportunity, but it requires self-reflection and careful consideration. By evaluating your strengths, setting meaningful career goals, and understanding your deeper motivations, you can confidently decide whether this career path aligns with your vision for the future.

If you've taken the time to assess where you're at, where you want to go, and why this career is important to you, you'll be well-equipped to make an informed decision—and take the next step in your journey.

Section 4.2: Planning Your Transition

You're almost at the end of this book, and soon you'll be ready to make the decision—**is becoming a Virtual Assistant right for you?** If you've made it this far, you're already well on your way. Now, it's time to think about how to plan your transition into this exciting career. The following steps will help you prepare for success, so you can smoothly move from where you are now to where you want to be.

1. Building a Financial Cushion

Starting a new career often means there will be an initial period where things aren't fully established yet. That's why having a financial cushion is so important. It'll help you manage your transition with less stress and more confidence.

- **Set aside savings**: Aim for 2-3 months' worth of living expenses to cover yourself during the early stages of your VA career.
- **Start part-time**: If you're currently employed, consider transitioning slowly by taking on small VA projects during evenings or weekends. This way, you can build your client base while still having income from your current job.
- **Track your expenses**: Understand your financial needs and budget carefully as you make this shift. Keep your expenses lean and manageable, especially during the early days of your VA career.

Having a financial cushion will help you feel more secure as you transition into your new role, so you can focus on growing your VA business without worrying about your finances.

2. Preparing Your Workspace

Creating a productive and comfortable workspace is essential to your success as a Virtual Assistant. Whether you're working from home full-time or part-time, having a space that encourages focus and efficiency can make a big difference.

- **Designate a specific area**: Set up a dedicated workspace, separate from other areas of your home, to help you mentally transition into work mode.
- **Invest in the right tools**: Ensure you have the equipment and software needed to do your job efficiently—such as a reliable computer, fast internet, and the productivity tools you'll use daily.

- **Eliminate distractions**: Create a quiet environment by minimizing distractions. This may include turning off social media notifications, using noise-canceling headphones, or setting clear boundaries with family or housemates during work hours.

A dedicated workspace will not only boost your productivity, but also help you maintain a clear distinction between your work and personal life.

3. Crafting a Clear Roadmap

Now that you've set the stage with your financial cushion and workspace, it's time to create a clear roadmap for your journey ahead. A roadmap will help you stay on track, prioritize your tasks, and keep moving toward your goals.

- **Define your immediate next steps**: What do you need to do to get started—whether it's setting up a website, creating profiles on freelance platforms, or networking? Break these steps down into actionable tasks.
- **Set short-term goals**: In the first few months, focus on building your client base, gaining experience, and refining your skills.
- **Create long-term goals**: Where do you want to be in 1 year or 5 years? Whether it's increasing your rates, specializing in a niche, or hiring a team, having long-term goals will help guide your decisions and keep you motivated.

Your roadmap will give you direction, helping you measure

progress and stay motivated, even when the journey feels overwhelming.

Keep Going—You're Almost There!

Planning your transition to becoming a Virtual Assistant takes time, but with each step you take, you're getting closer to your goal. Remember, the transition doesn't happen overnight, but with a financial cushion, a well-prepared workspace, and a clear roadmap, you'll be set up for success.

You've almost finished this book—**keep reading and finish strong!** By the time you reach the end, you'll have all the tools and knowledge you need to confidently decide if becoming a VA is the right career path for you.

Section 4.3: Making the Final Decision

First off, **congratulations** for making it this far! You've put in the time to learn, reflect, and evaluate your potential as a Virtual Assistant. This is a big step, and it's exciting to know that you're on the verge of making a decision that could change the course of your career.

Now, before you make the final leap, it's time to weigh the pros and cons, conduct a reality check, and ultimately decide if becoming a VA is right for you. Pay close attention, because this is an important decision that will shape your future.

1. Weighing Pros and Cons

At this stage, you probably have a good understanding of what becoming a VA entails. It's time to evaluate everything you've learned so far. Consider what excites you about this career path—and what challenges you might face.

- **Pros of becoming a VA**:
- Flexible schedule
- Opportunity to work from anywhere
- Diverse range of industries and clients
- Ability to choose niches that align with your interests
- Potential for growth and scalability
- **Cons of becoming a VA**:
- Initial challenges in finding clients
- Setting up a business (if you're going solo)
- Possible periods of inconsistency in workload or income
- Self-discipline is required to stay productive

By comparing the pros and cons, you'll have a clearer picture of how this career could align with your personal goals and lifestyle.

2. Conducting a Reality Check

It's easy to get caught up in the excitement of a new opportunity, but now it's time to be real with yourself. Take a moment to honestly assess the practical aspects of this career path.

- **Financial stability**: Do you have the financial cushion to

make the transition? Will you be able to sustain yourself during the early stages of finding clients?
- **Time commitment**: Can you commit the time needed to build your VA business, especially if you're starting part-time while working another job?
- **Skills and readiness**: Are you prepared to handle the technical, communication, and self-management skills required to succeed as a VA?

Being honest with yourself about these realities will help you make a grounded decision.

3. Taking the Leap

Now that you've reflected on the pros and cons and conducted a reality check, it's time to take the leap. **This is the moment where you trust your judgment** and decide whether you're ready to commit.

- **If you're ready**: Congratulations! Take your roadmap, start setting goals, and begin the process of building your business. It's time to get started on this exciting new path.
- **If you're not quite sure**: That's okay. Sometimes it takes a bit more time to figure things out. If you need to sharpen your skills or gain more confidence, that's perfectly fine. Take a step back, reassess, and continue your journey at your own pace.

You've Done It—Now Decide

Making the decision to become a Virtual Assistant is no small feat. **Good job for getting this far!** You've gathered the information, evaluated your skills, and now it's time to make an empowered choice. Whether you're ready to dive into this new career or need a little more time to prepare, remember this—**you are in control**.

Take a deep breath, trust your instincts, and decide with confidence. The journey is yours to shape.

Conclusion

As you come to the end of *The Virtual Assistant Starter Handbook*, you're standing at an important crossroads. Whether you're about to take the leap into the world of virtual assistance or still weighing your options, the most important thing is that you've learned and grown during this process.

Let's quickly recap the key points we've covered in the book:

- **Chapter 1: Understanding the Virtual Assistant Role** – You now have a clear understanding of what a VA does, the scope of the work, and the industries that rely on VAs. This foundation is key as you move forward.
- **Chapter 2: Skills and Tools Every VA Needs** – From administrative to technical skills, and the essential tools you need, you now know what it takes to set yourself up for success as a VA.
- **Chapter 3: Exploring Opportunities and Finding Clients** – You've learned where to find clients and how to market yourself effectively. Building your client base is the crucial next step, and you now have the strategies to do so.
- **Chapter 4: Deciding if Becoming a VA is Right for You** – Finally, you've evaluated your strengths, set your goals, and

taken an honest look at the realities of becoming a VA. You're now equipped to make an informed decision about whether or not this career path is for you.

Whatever decision you make at the end of this book is a good one. The key is to keep moving forward. Whether you decide to take the plunge into the world of virtual assistance or pursue a different path, just remember—**as long as you keep going, keep improving, and never stay stagnant, you're on the right track.**

Your dream business is waiting for you. It may take time, it may take effort, but the journey will be worth it. Don't be afraid to take that first step, knowing you have everything you need to succeed.

If you've found this book helpful, I'd love to hear from you. Please take a moment to leave a review and share your thoughts. Your feedback helps others who are considering this exciting career journey, and it means the world to me.

Good luck on your VA journey—whatever you choose, the world is full of possibilities!

Resources:

1. Breeliance. (2024, May 13). THE DIFFERENT KINDS OF CLIENTS IN THE VA FIELD. Breeliance. https://www.breeliance.com/post/the-different-kinds-of-clients-in-the-

va-field
2. GatothoMBABSc, G. (2024, July 22). Key statistics revealing the growth of the virtual assistant industry. https://www.linkedin.com/pulse/key-statistics-revealing-growth-virtual-assistant-gladys-oajyf/
3. ATO - 20 Virtual Assistant Statistics you should know. (n.d.). https://www.ateamoverseas.com/blog-posts/20-virtual-assistant-statistics-you-should-know
4. Knight, R. (2024, March 13). How to improve your soft skills as a remote worker. Harvard Business Review. https://hbr.org/2024/01/how-to-improve-your-soft-skills-as-a-remote-worker

www.ingramcontent.com/pod-product-compliance
Lightning Source LLC
Chambersburg PA
CBHW070418230526
45471CB00006B/2873